Fraying Edge
of Sky

CODHILL

Also by Danielle Hanson

Ambushing Water

Fraying Edge *of* Sky

POEMS

Danielle Hanson

March 2019

CODHILL

Codhill Press
New Paltz, New York

CODHILL

Codhill books are published by David Appelbaum for Codhill Press

Book and cover design by Alicia Fox

ACKNOWLEDGMENTS

I am grateful to the editors of these journals, in which the following poems first appeared, sometimes in slightly different versions.

Adelaide: "A Poem in Which the Moon Rejects You," "Dear Heron," "Instructions on Stripping"
Apple Valley Review: "Forest Scene," "Nonlinearity"
The Atlanta Review: "Medusa as Vampire"
Badlands Poetry Journal: "How to Get Plural"
Blackbird: "Generations" (as *No Diga Mas Que Lo Que No Diga*"), "Near Sleep in a Smoky Room"
Blue Lake Review: "Fingers Leaving a Woman"
Clackamas Literary Review: "Saints"
The Cortland Review: "The Escaping Soul"
Eureka Literary Magazine: "Ticks"
Folly: "The Ice Skater"
Homestead Review: "The House"
Hubbub: "Metamorphosis"
*isacoustic: "Ant Curse," "Urban Renewal"
Lingerpost: "The Effect of Rip Van Winkle on His Neighbors," "The Sparrow"
The Meadow: "Carving a Name in the Ice of a River," "Howling"
Peacock Journal: "As He Is Reading a Letter from Her," "Leda," "Love Song"
Pennsylvania Literary Journal: "In Order to Be a Good Angel, You Must Think Like the Devil"
Poet Lore: "Batting Average"
Quail Bell Review: "The Constancy of Light," "The Lake"
Red River Review: "The Zombie Minotaur"
Roanoke Review: "Free Radicals"
Sulphur River Literary Review: "Hourglass"
Temenos Journal: "Lunacy"
The Texas Review: "To You, Beautiful Old Woman"
Thin Air: "Coatimundi"

"Metamorphosis" earned the 2016 Vi Gale Award from *Hubbub*

for Magnus, Olivia, Annika

CONTENTS

I

A Guide to Ridding Oneself of an Infestation of Angels   3

Dismantling an Angel   4

Instructions on Stripping   5

The Secret Doors   6

List of Confessions   7

A Poem in Which the Moon Rejects You   8

Time Lapse   9

The Ant Curse   10

A Thousand White Insects   11

Saints   12

The Constancy of Light   13

Howling   14

The Hydra as Mummy   15

Nature   16

The Zombie Minotaur   17

Leda   18

The Gods Have Deserted Us   19

How to Build a Bird   20

The Experiment   21

Exhale   22

II

A Piece of Fog Like a Ribbon   25

The Tailor   26

Angels as Mice   27

List of Things to Be Imagined   28

The Lake   29

Signs   30

The House   31

Dear Heron   32

Near Sleep in a Smoky Room   33

The Effect of Rip Van Winkle on His Neighbors   34

Love Song 35

As He Is Reading a Letter from Her 36

Nonlinearity 37

Inventory 38

Urban Renewal 39

In Order to Be a Good Angel, You Must Think Like a Devil 40

Lunacy 41

Free Radicals 42

Brisk 43
Exodus, Urban 44

III

The Light Is Calling the Shadows 47

Coatimundi 48

The Sparrow 49

Who Are You 50

Forest Scene 51

Carving a Name in the Ice of a River 52

The Ice Skater 53

Fingers Leaving a Woman 54

Ticks 55

Plagues of Angels 56

Metamorphosis 57

Hourglass 58

Generations 59

Batting Average 60

How to Get Plural 61

Dr. Frankenstein at It Again 62

The Escaping Soul 63

Medusa as a Vampire 64

Bette Midler on World Tour 65

To You, Beautiful Old Woman 66

Recycling the Angels 67

About the Author 69

He seemed to be in so many places at the same time that they grew to think that he'd been duplicated, that he was reproducing himself all through the house, and the exasperated and unhinged Elisenda shouted that it was awful living in that hell full of angels.

—GABRIEL GARCÍA MÁRQUEZ,
"A Very Old Man with Enormous Wings"

I

A Guide to Ridding Oneself of an Infestation of Angels

Handpicking is best—
a gentle squeeze
between forefinger
and thumb.

Dismantling an Angel

You can't start with the wings,
but something smaller and less angelic,
an arm, for example, or an ear.
You must remove the hair, if it exists—
    although who ever wanted a hairy angel?
Then remove the flesh, a lantern
slowly burning out.
You are left with only a bone—
    but what is the bone of an angel?
It is the sound of air through a cave.
Let it float away over the hill.
Then turn your attention to the next.

Instructions on Stripping

Take the rotten unused light of the moon,
add what the mirror sees when it is dark—
        forgetting is lovely at night.
Throw away all that you were
into the opposite of wind.
Pretend to be a ghost.
Now pretend to be a rock.
What have you learned about permanence?

The Secret Doors

The secret doors of Heaven open
as if they could dismantle all we've done,
as if the water in the jars could become sweet again
after turning bitter from our angry words last night.
Pick up the shards of them, poor shadows.
Hold them up to the light dripping in from the window.
Let them rest and then circle overhead.
Let us become the meadow to their hawk.

List of Confessions

I left a mirror hidden in the shadows
to trap the sun. I held the moon
under water and watched her drown.
I stapled a spider to the sky,
and then another, and then another
in the outline of you.
I practiced getting lost so I could lead you astray.
I captured your words in a jar with vinegar.
I pickled your words.
I made your words into a condiment.
I am slowly replacing you
with hair I collect from your pillow.
I forgot to take a picture of your absence.
I deleted the picture I took of your absence.

A Poem in Which the Moon Rejects You

In the photograph of what is gone,
the one that is not an omen,
the one that leaned too far into the light
and shattered it,
the photo in which the world is reduced
to a shard, in the shard
which reflects only the moon,
in the light cast off by that moon,
lost light, falling light.

Time Lapse

Watch the flowers open and close with the light.
Watch them chew the air. Watch them eat lies. You,
angel of lies and of night.
Rilke said, *every angel is terrible,*
but he is the light that lies through its teeth.
Press your silk to my whisper.
Cover yourself in my ashes.
Curl our edges inwards, paper burning.

The Ant Curse

I attach a curse to ant,
whisper your name in its ear.
Memories are like ghosts
you can't look in the eye.
The dead have their own
tasks, lists that always
begin with departure.
Are you dead yet?
There is *ant*
that is *curse*
looking for you.

A Thousand White Insects

The light behind you is crumbling into a thousand white insects.
Not able to see your face, I feel it must be changing to a giant moth
or another simple angel stumbling upward.
The news tonight talked of war splintering into a thousand tiny battles.
I'm scared. I'm looking for infinity.
There's a single fungus in Washington State that has grown to over two miles.
It's searching for infinity too.
According to mathematics, infinity could be anywhere, waiting to ambush.
One day a girl decided to search for Heaven, another infinity.
Her body was found fifteen floors below. According to the mathematician Riemann,
infinity is found on a sphere, opposite zero, like boring to the South Pole.
I heard witnesses at the scene say she walked upward.
She may be one casualty and you, another. One general was quoted,
"Shoot them all and let Heaven sort them out."

Saints

The benefit of being stone is that time
slows. Take the saints on church tops,
eternal contemplation of a jump. They
look down on the tourists, on me, the occupants
of Dante's First Level. The saints feel superior
for their height and their depth—
the Seventh Circle is for them, the eternal
wood of suicides. The saints think for centuries,
first of the step, then of the fall,
then of the scattering of stone.
They wonder if angels fell
with the speed of gravity or if they
fell like seeds. They wonder if angels
would scatter, if angels have atoms,
if angels are liquid, if angels feel at home
above the Ninth Level. They wonder if they can aim,
could land on me, could watch me scatter and seep
through to Styx to be washed up among the pagans.
They wonder if the street will stop their fall.
They hope the momentum will carry them far,
scatter them wide, stir enough dust into the wind
become breath, never landing.

The Constancy of Light

If, as was said by the ancient Eriphes,
the amount of light in the world is constant,
the creation of the candle was a pebble
dislodged from a stone dam,
and the light bulb has brought
the draining of the soul. Come,
blanket of earth. Cover me.
The sky is wide open. I cannot breathe.

Howling

The howling of dogs swirls
on the wind tonight. I bury it
as quickly as possible.
The only sentence you can say
in this language is a lie.
Lie down—lie still
while I cover you with earth,
dear shadow. If the stones
shred you, I will offer your pieces
to the sun. I will chant
prayers to you in an unearthed tongue.

The Hydra as a Mummy

The hydra is a mummy, but how did it become that way?
Let's say Hercules has already dispatched the monster,
leaving a stump to be wrapped tight as a seed in its hull,
each head stored in a Coptic jar—an endless stack in a tomb.
When the tomb is disturbed, the mummy wanders forth,
headless, eyeless, slow.
Does the hydra return to water?
Wet bandages, moldering, waterlogged?
But let's say the hydra did not belong to Hercules.
Perhaps it wilted with age, each head wrapped individually,
spiced with cedar, juniper, henna,
laid in a many-headed coffin inside coffin.
And when the mummy exits, and the modern archeological hero
cuts off head after head, new live ones sprout in their places.
A flower blooming after a harsh winter.

Nature

There's a law of nature
that in winter
returns the sound
of our feet
hitting the ice.

And there are times
when things
get mixed up,
when in summer
the sound of running
makes us sad.
It leads to empty houses.

It's what makes
a woman want
to push
away her own baby, crawl
out of her belly
and begin again.

It is the feeling
that makes a man
envy the cowboy,
know that walking
into sunsets like walls
is a way of embracing
emptiness. It is the feeling
that makes a man glad
he is not a cowboy.

And perhaps it is the feeling
that makes a bird fly
toward the sun,
chasing the idea of sun.

The Zombie Minotaur

The Zombie Minotaur is shuffling
around his cell. He does not want
fourteen young victims. He only wants
brains. These are not filling.
The Zombie Minotaur is wasting
away, confused. Every pathway
leads to turns. He walks into
wall after wall.

Leda

She always leaves a bite of her dinner for her guardian angel. That's her mistake. He finally comes. He eats the bite. He doesn't stop. He eats the plate. He eats the table. He eats air one vapor at a time, starting with the water. It's suddenly a desert in her mind. He doesn't stop.

Her legs spread like wings, like she can't control them. The fur of her body becomes feathers. She is not an angel, she is a bird flying in this vacuum, being flown, being flung backwards, air ripped apart by wind.

The Gods Have Deserted Us

The gods have deserted us
like migrating birds,
like grain moths startled from meal,
like hundreds of insects exposed to the light,
like lizards escaping the forest on fire.
The gods have deserted us, taking the sun.

The gods have deserted us
like migrating birds.
The winter gods have moved in
with their feathers puffed against cold
and their snow-hushed voices.
The winter gods are focused on survival.
We offer them suet and seed.

The gods have deserted us
like migrating birds.
At last we are free from their noise.
Their excrement ceases to cover our lands.
We can at last raise our heads to the sky.

How to Build a Bird

Start with a balloon inflated with sky,
filter out the clouds—moisture adds weight.
Water always seeks the ground.
Attach leaves for feathers—gingko wings,
elm tail. It is tempting
to use sticks for feet, but only ones
picked fresh from the highest branches.
Remember, this is a golem of sky.
The beak should be a sprouting seed of grass.
And how does it fly? Whisper to it,
The earth is full of eyes.

The Experiment

Collect light in a bucket of water,
pour it off slowly—keep the light
from breaking, watch it seep into soil.
Now it is dark;
time to get rid of the night.
Dig a hole to drain it.
See how the hole already brims over
with darkness, saturated.
Dig deeper, with more urgency.
Mine the blackness. Keep pushing
until fog rises up.
Realize you are nothing.

Exhale

How the fog last night came in thick.
How the windows this morning were covered with it.
How it refused to leave.
How it wrapped us up as liquid mummies.
How the power went out and darkness joined forces to bury us.
How we escaped to the street and stood there, outside ourselves.
    Zombies instead of mummies, a more useful kind of dead.

II

A Piece of Fog Like a Ribbon

I picked it up
and whipped
the dog of your love.

The Tailor

He starts by sewing the fraying
edge of sky to a rock.
Catching a frog,
he sews it in as well, what
a wonderful patch—moisture
to make fog out of amphibian.
A small mouse walks by
and becomes progenitor
of all miniature fuzzy flying creatures—
gnats and flies and the smallest moths.
The tailor gets carried away,
begins sewing lizards, squirrels, opossums
to the sky. He creates
a daytime field of constellations,
embroidery of a new creation.

Angels as Mice

The infestation was in the crawl
space and walls—chanting
under floorboards, hosannas in
the middle of night,
angel scat in the yard at dawn.
The websites said to take action
at the first sign, so we set
traps and waited.
If the infestation goes on long enough
you may start to notice a distinct
unpleasant smell, markings
on the wall—angels leave grease trails
wherever they go, spreading diseases
to smite the wicked,
announcing unwanted pregnancies.
If you find angels, don't try cohabitating.
We patch holes in floors and stop
prayers for intersession. Dispose
of bodies, double-bagged. Keep pets
away. We make conditions inhospitable—
avoid being the only holy people in an unclean town,
or prophets slacking their duties. We must stop
being shepherds watching flocks at night.

List of Things to Be Imagined

A flashlight for viewing darkness as itself,
    staring at you from across the bedstead.
A language which can crack stones.
The dissection of a mythical creature, griffin or faun.
A walking stampede, slow and terrible.
The hospital for nonexistent children.
A mountain devouring the clouds.
Your memory of me, silverfish between yellow pages.

The Lake

A lake formed when she looked away—
    this was fiction but who created it?
She did not see the earth suck in its belly
or pull down the water from the clouds.
She was walking away when time dropped
second by second as fish,
and a tadpole of neglect leaked from shore.
Let the lake grasses be weak and bent.
Let the geese fly past without pause.
Let the snails be malformed and dry.
    This is not a dream lake after all.

Signs

Now is the time to look for signs. The land
is on fire, it actually is, and what could this mean?
That her sad eyes cut thin slices of lemon for tea?
That the water is constantly collapsing, sacrificing
form like a monk, or the dead? Or that
a fish is unbraiding river, letting if fall
loose on the bank's shoulders, an exhausted
lover lying down? That a hawk is a hungry angel,
circling? This is its shadow across a page.

The House

He died on Wednesday and the house
began to decompose.
The walls thinned slowly
until only the studs showed.
In ancient South Africa, bodies were buried,
dug up, and placed in pottery jars like food.
This house wasn't even buried once,
which may seem a sign:
Is the house unloved?
But this is the culture of houses,
religion of rust, microorganisms,
being consumed by the small.
The opposite of nirvana, just as sweet.

Dear Heron

You have grown tired of my presence.
I am a ghost haunting the wrong house.
You are the knowing inhabitant of my ineffectiveness.
I am what happens in the hour when clocks fall forward.
I am a lost hour of spring.
In fall, I am erased.
Have no regrets—migrate from my absence!
I will remain as a black rock rolling over in water,
as a ghost bound to earth,
as the weight of honey-soaked feathers,
as the stones eaten by birds to crush their feed.
You will remain the night, rising from the earth at dawn.

Near Sleep in a Smoky Room

The smoke is building something large and hollow,
with a door opening to oranges.
I stop hearing what's being said
over the sound of the light buzzing.
I say the light is a giant bug. I say
the light is an alarm clock to the air.
I say the air needs to awaken. I say the dream
of the air is over. I say I can hear now.
The words are the kind of bridge bodies are found under.
A tour group is invading the castle behind my eyes.
The trees in my ribs are growing.
My breath is negative presence.
My ears are smuggling themselves across borders in boxes
made to hold bananas.
The tarantulas are nibbling the lobes.
A man unpacks them, puts them on a shelf, three pounds for a dollar.
They're still green while a redhead with breasts of ice cream
places them gently into her cart.
At home a man is waiting for her, waiting for bananas,
waiting for ice cream.
He looks at the window's thoughts.
They caress him, drag him, make him forget everything
about the sea and the clouds, remember only land.
He sees a building being made of fog.

The Effect of Rip Van Winkle on His Neighbors

The man rumbled out of town one day, my sleep tucked away in his pack along with a loaf of bread from the counter and a newspaper. The first night, I thought I must have misplaced sleep. I checked bed, recliner, hammock, floor. I began hearing rumors of Rip and his slumber.

Over the years I visited Rip—glaring at him, putting bugs into his snoring mouth, kicking and prodding, anything to wake him so that I could grab sleep and run. When the wind carried the dark smell of roots, I laid in the cellar, arms and toes curled, fists full of dreams.

Love Song

The cat of you has been stalking my eyes all morning,
as startling as waking up on the other side of night
without Cerberus still at your throat.
Would you believe, after all this, that I love you—
    oh, all is lost!
The way a glass melts to your hand while I watch,
the sun going down in a bottle,
like the way your bare skin shines in moonlight
while the stars take flight overhead.
Your touch is the door that opens everything,
a door to a constantly shifting sea.
The river is wearing galoshes.
I've been learning a lost language
by listening to your thoughts.
But when I look for my lips, I must look to your mouth.

As He Is Reading a Letter from Her

The precise hour after sunset when
the shadows have not yet completed their
slow coil around the clear presence of things.

— PESSOA

Another glorious night is being born out of the wreckage—
the crash and burn of the sun. The time of small lights is upon us.
St. Elmo's fires play soccer over the sea of distant thoughts.
The ignition of longing. Let me fuse
with distant skin, electric,
the skin over the aura of the earth.

Nonlinearity

He says, "You're a non sequitur,"
and I suddenly feel the way birds must feel
when they wake in the morning
and realize they're not on solid ground.
He says, "I'll explain it again,"
and tells me how the moon dissolves
during a lunar eclipse.
His voice sounds like he swallowed sandpaper.
I think of how the sand in the desert
bakes to make a mirror of the sun.
He's telling me about gravity and light.
I tell him I'm a gravitational catalyst.
Things always fall around me.
He's not listening.
Now he's on to describing cannibalistic solar systems
while my thoughts devour themselves before hatching.
The dinosaurs died that way.
He doesn't notice this thought
leaking out on my shoulder, making me nervous.
I tell him I'm lost between freezing and melting.
I ask for directions but he tells me a flower opens
with all the force of an atom and drains the sun.
I'm worried about gardens.
I ask him about constancy of light.

Inventory

In the training of astronauts,
a plane simulates loss
of gravity,
dips then falls into sky
following the trail
of any rejected thing.
It's throwing
yourself at the ground
and finding out you can fly.
Weightlessness causes motion—
this is my second
coffee shop today.
This place is quiet
and goes better with my socks.
Time has slowed and
I can feel the change
in my pocket adding weight
to my thigh. I take it out
and count it. I count it
again and again enjoying
the counting, the cloth of
repetition until
another contrail
pulls the tail of my attention.

Urban Renewal

Let's look at that empty lot over there,
where liquor store with more dust
and rust than bottles once stood.
Let's imagine it as field—let's cover it
with flowers—purples, blues, reds,
and enough yellow to make us squint a little.
And let's inscribe each petal with a fortune,
or the name of a past lover, or a secret involving
blood and lots of it. Let's use the most expensive
inks, set types lost since the Middle Ages.
Then let's light it up—let's watch
flora ghosts rising from a field on fire.

In Order to Be a Good Angel, You Must Think Like the Devil

If the sky is a dome above us, as Eriphes claimed,
then it must, like Icarus' wings, be made of wax
melting by the sun and dripping to the oceans,
the Ring of Fire (the border of the Pacific) being the wicks.

But this cannot be true, for we know
the moon is the center of the universe.
That accounts for day and night—light, of course,
being a fluid pouring in and out of the drain
of stars as the earth makes its daily revolution.
Shadows are stars turned inside out, the proof being
that each of us is dark inside, a refrigerator
with a burned-out light.

The motivating force is the gravity of darkness,
a vertigo of sorts. Light is drawn to retreating darkness
like cold to hot, causing a wind
while rushing forward only to turn back on itself,
a luminous tsunami leaving the puddle-moon and starfish,
those parts of the night which overslept,
cousins of black holes digging in gardens of nightshade.

It is as Eriphes in his lesser-known theory said:
we are all cold inside,
refrigerators—each of us a tiny model for Dante's sculpting,
each of us holding Judas in his teeth, pulled down
into the center of darkness, inside the moon,
past the icy wind, through the stars with light flowing,
crashing as our wings melt, swimming in the bowl of sky.

Lunacy

I'm tying myself to the earth
with the roots of small things:
tomatoes, herbs, moonflower.
Moon, make something of yourself.
You are a kite. Tether yourself and
be still, grow downward.
You are your own gravitational mass.
Moon, make rivers. Create *flood*.

Free Radicals

Who could have known the rain
would last for days and we'd be trapped
inside our heads with flies
until words well up in their noise?
Death is a slow rusting, they say
and I wonder about the toxicity of waterproofing.

Everything is wearing down slowly in the rain.
Everything is being misplaced—
the yard is in the house,
the clouds are sinking into the ground,
nothing floats.

I want to lift up like levitations at a carnival.
I want to saw everything in half,
run swords through a snakecharmer's basket,
carve up the basket,
part for a flyswatter, the rest an umbrella.

Brisk

So cold it was only possible to exhale—
eyeballs crawled out of their lair
to resettle in the burrow of my mouth.
They were followed by the nose,
running, of course, to the warmth.
Fingers and toes joined the migration,
chased by the new extremities of ankles and wrists—
then arms, legs, skin,
until there was nothing left in the cold.
The flowers could bloom in this new springtime.
The sun high above the earth.

Exodus, Urban

First came the plague of rats,
then the plague of dead rat stench.
Along with it came the plague of flies,
big, fat, covering.
Then the plague of dead flies
accompanied by the plague of decomposition-too-small-to-see,
followed by the death of those.
The plagues have grown smaller, but larger in multitude
and we have—in the vacuum—grown larger.
We are giants over the fallen.

III

The Light Is Calling the Shadows

out to play,
ambushing them.

Coatimundi

In early morning, I see you.
You may be groggy, like me.
You may be tired, waddling off to bed.
It's always dark under this
sky of trees. I can't imagine
you lifting your nose to see it,
half its bulbs burned out, half-light.
I fear I do not know you.

You are the room made of clay from my dream,
dusty, forgotten, and folding
in on itself like bread being kneaded,
stretched under a rolling pin,
wheels over macadam then gone.

I believe you to be deaf, your ears chaste.
I believe you cannot believe.
I see your one thought rattling
against your eyes like a moth stuck
inside a window.
I don't even know myself.

The Sparrow

> *A bat, discovered in England ten years after her*
> *species was declared extinct, talks to the press*

Today I am a sparrow. Tomorrow I may be a squirrel. The day after possibly a dog. I have studied creatures for years and am qualified to be any of them. Today, I am a sparrow. I have accomplished all the sparrow tasks. I have a nest, which I have brought with me today for your examination. I have eaten bugs (you might point out that other species, such as bats, eat bugs but I assure you that the manner in which I ate them was extremely sparrow-like). I have sung on-key and ceaselessly. I have flitted from branch to wire and am willing to demonstrate to you. Today, as you can see, I am a sparrow. I am not alone.

Who Are You

Who are you to hold the throat of the world in your fist,
to be the taste of words swallowed not spoken?
I shine a light on your shadows to see them more clearly,
but they splinter like night into crows, into murder.
You have choked the sky into the color
of a drowned child's wrist in a river.
I take your name and throw it into that river,
a word that breaks stones.

Forest Scene

The forest grows silent.
All that remains
is the gurgling a spring makes
while being choked by rocks.

If you hide from these forces,
they will sometimes pass you by.

A lizard pretends to be stone.
A bird pretends to be leaf.
A mountain pretends
to be the throne of God.

A cloud passes over,
a rowboat.

Carving a Name in the Ice of a River

It would be pointless if you didn't need a knife.
Be careful not to slip—you won't feel the pain,
but your work will be as undone as your heart.
Now sit back and shiver—wait until spring.
Freeze slowly to your death as the name unmoors.
It is off to haunt the ocean. You cannot haunt the ocean.

The Ice Skater

This is on TV—
old woman skating
alone, dressed
as a ballerina.
There is no commentary,
although this is the local news,
no byline, no sign
around her neck saying,
"You, I am dancing for
you." I am the lost,
an omen
butterfly at night
posing as a moth,
mad light.

Fingers Leaving a Woman

> *Here we have stopped giving*
> *The dying good wine.*
> *We have stopped calling them.*
>   —ERIPHES

It started with a light,
the forces of angels colliding,
fate kidnapped from her bed.
Somewhere a storm
overtakes the land even as it runs.
Here time stands as a broken clock.
It's 3 'til 8. It's always 3 'til 8.
I've been awake,
my dreams have melted,
the puddle dried.
The coffeemaker is broken.
My body brews.
We slip in and out of time.
We are clothes leaving a woman,
fingers strumming guitar strings.
True, things lost reappear.
But we would gladly exchange
missing for forgetting.

Ticks

I've been thinking about you all day,
not the book I'm reading or
the ticks I've pulled off the dog.
I can see your eyes from the other side of the city
as if they're watching me.
If you were here, I would want you without speaking.
Then I would tell you everything until I was empty.
I'd be a tick, alive and waiting for you in the woods.
Or you'd be the tick—you seem to know it so well,
the burrowing, the sucking, the dying as you crawl off.
I know the itch and blood of the wound.

Plagues of Angels

    I. The angels turn to blood. The river stinks. You cannot drink it.

   II. The country teams with angels. They come into your house and onto your bed. They crawl into your ovens.

  III. The angels infest your heads. They itch.

  IV. It is unclear whether the angels are wild animals or flies. It is clear the angels bite.

   V. The angels are a virus in your livestock's blood.

  VI. Angels erupt under your skin.

 VII. Angels flash in the sky. Their falling tramples crops.

VIII. The hungry angels eat what is left in the fields.

  IX. The angels grow so fat they block the sun for three days.

   X. Your firstborn have become the angels.

Metamorphosis

The blue-eyed angel of San Marco,
pigeon on her back,
wings spread, eyes raised,
warns me to run from the garden's rain,
so fine it feels like little
more than air falling.

"Santo, Santo, Santo," call my shoes
fearing the echo will be
"Tosan, Tosan. Everything's backwards."

The rain is making me think this.
Or the stones under my feet.
Or the people passing so fast I can feel
the death in them.
All I can remember
is the blackness of the room
and the way the incense
flicked ashes of itself onto
the bedside table.
That time is a crab.

Hourglass

Light is the sand.
The last of it is falling through the window
and with it, night.

The stars become fireflies, then
melt into ground. Stars
and memory are sticking and
I need a bath.

The time is held in candles,
too heavy, a dust on tomorrow like so much else.
No energy to clean; I must leave myself alone

while I get something to wear,
listen to the crickets and night birds
though what do they, prey
of the dawn, know about anything?

Generations

The trees weep, their needles
dropping and tumbling like liquid,
a constant realignment of beards.
Trees migrate, but over generations.
Each succession reaching new heights
against a coming ice age.
The mountains these trees cry above are large
and numerous. No people have seen all their sides.
Their untamed parts don't know their own savagery.
They move nowhere, stalk nothing.
They have a sunny side and a dark. Both are silent.
Both spend days staring into lakes like Narcissus.
These lakes reflect nothing but the mountains
and a hawk. They are deep with fish.
The fish on the sunny side sun themselves in the shallows.
The fish of shadow only watch the giant bird whose wings
spread before the sun. The bird is watching
for a fish large enough to make the dive.
The fish live in fear, hope never to grow.
They hide in algae that drips like beards and never moves.

Batting Average

The escape velocity of an object from earth is seven miles per second.
The boy sharing this lake wishes he could throw rocks that fast.
It's obvious from the baseball card collection he pulls out
from under the trees that his hero is Rob Dibble.
He can only throw 102 miles per hour or .03 miles per second. The power
to overcome gravity is the power to rid oneself
of an object forever.

The boy concentrates on the bluegills and reflected trees.
It is hard to tell which is where.
Everything is far away and mysterious and changes
more often than the wind on water.

Galileo made his measurements using
his pulse. Galileo must never have
known love or he could not have predicted
the flight of a baseball hit at a
thirty-degree angle with an initial velocity of
a bluegill's flight through branches—not
even fast enough to escape a small moon.

At this the boy leaves.

I look up and the sky is
smiling over him like a wolf at the kill.

How to Get Plural

When electrons in a particle accelerator race together,
their pieces splatter to the tracing screen
like blood on the wall in a cheap
horror movie. The light's on but no one's home.
In a tight grove of trees a light can make
an inverted shadow in the dark leaves.
From there it's a short walk to nowhere.
Hitchhiking isn't advisable.
Life is smuggling itself over death's border.
Many ideas are traveling in the air like birds
barely missing each other.
In the church they light a candle for life
and another for death. But life's candles have fallen
from their swings. The sun has been blown to other places.
The renegade shadows make the water.
A man walked around the world for a shoe ad
stopping only at the oceans where water casts to itself.

Dr. Frankenstein at It Again

He has sewn three heads to a dog,
and it is terrible—a beast bound straight to Hell,
angry in three heads at once.
He has grafted a stag to a lion,
 a lion to a bird,
 a bird to a woman.
He pauses from his work and admires the woman.
He tweaks—replacing one part with another,
transforms the harpy into an angel with swan's wings,
turns Hell into Heaven and rests.

The Escaping Soul

I couldn't catch my soul when I sneezed last week.
The glue of *Gesundheit* has gotten old
and cracked in its bottle.
I tried everything to get it back,
a Dustbuster, a Hoover when that didn't work.
It had used a crowbar to escape.
I lost two teeth. I wanted to put up fliers
offering a reward, but couldn't find its picture.
I think it may now be on the road with the gypsies of America,
who believe that pictures steal a person's soul.
Gypsies steal souls. My soul was entranced by their freedom, it always hated
being stuck inside a person like me who knew the scam
behind four kids and a flat tire. There were guys at my high school
who always asked for lunch money. Some days they made twenty dollars.
My soul would make a killing doing that. The little tramp
always knew how to use her eyes. She'll fit in well.

Medusa as a Vampire

Medusa is not a good vampire,
despite the fangs in her hair.
With a look, she turns men into stone,
impenetrable necks, frozen blood.
She has tried closing her eyes,
but no one stands still
and waits for a vampire.

Medusa never looked sexy in a cape,
even when she wore nothing underneath it.
"Hey, my eyes are up here."
But she meant it as a failed warning.

Medusa's head is on Athena's shield,
although she's undead.
A bat has flown from her severed body
in the form of a winged horse.
Laughable monster, pitiful really.

Bette Midler on World Tour

She steps out of a hot dog costume, and why not?
Why would Venus only emerge from a giant clam?
Why not burst through the fake intestinal case
of a sausage?
    Would the smell be any worse?
Why limit oneself to the seashore
with its shoveling children
and view-obstructing umbrellas? No—
Venus should emerge in a stadium,
an audience of pumped-up men cheering,
goddess of lust and meat.

To You, Beautiful Old Woman

To you, beautiful
old woman
sitting in your doorway
in Monteriggioni
under the Tuscan sun.
You, who sat
still for a photo.
You, who would have
sat still
regardless.
You, ripe
from the Tuscan sun.
By the wall
only possibly
older than you,
ancient one.
In your pink sweater,
human fig,
woman,
in an ancient
chair from
your one room
in the medieval wall.
You, who have
outlived all
that was yours.
You, who have outlived
family, trees, wars,
your doorway
open, you soaking
up the sun
in Monteriggioni,
ancient Etruscan
outliving your gods.

Recycling the Angels

They must be sorted, of course—
    seraphim, cherubim, and arch—
rinsed out, insides scraped if needed.
Soak them in soap. Contamination
is a major concern. Eternity
is long and resources limited.
Repurposed, an angel of death
can be a composting vessel.
A guardian angel keeps vermin
from the crops. Singing angels
make good alarms. Fallen angels,
salvageable for parts—wind,
fire, wax—can repair gently-used angels,
markdowns at consignment shops.
To waste an angel is a terrible thing.

ABOUT THE AUTHOR

Danielle Hanson earned an MFA from Arizona State University and has held residencies at The Hambidge Center in Rabun Gap, Georgia. Author of *Ambushing Water* (Brick Road Poetry Press, 2017) and 2016 recipient of the Vi Gale Award from *Hubbub,* her poems have appeared widely, including in *Asheville Poetry Review, The Atlanta Review, Blackbird, Borderlands, The Cortland Review, Hiram Poetry Review, Mudfish, Poetry East, Poet Lore, Roanoke Review, Rosebud, Verse Daily,* and *Willow Springs.* She is poetry editor for Doubleback Books, has edited *Loose Change Magazine* and *Hayden's Ferry Review,* and has been a staff member at the Meacham Writers' Conference and the Chattahoochee Valley Writers' Conference.